Osvaldo Golijov

Ainadamar

Libretto by David Henry Hwang

(Choral and Off-stage Voices)

Choral Score

HENDON MUSIC

BOOSEY & HAWKES

AN IMAGEM COMPANY

DISTRIBUTED BY

HAL•LEONARD®
CORPORATION
7777 W. BLUEMOUND RD. P.O. BOX 13819 MILWAUKEE, WI 53213

www.boosey.com
www.halleonard.com

Published by Hendon Music, Inc.
a Boosey & Hawkes company
229 West 28th Street, 11th Floor
New York NY 10001

www.boosey.com

First Printing, 2003
Second Printing, 2009
Third Printing, newly engraved, 2012

Cover painting by Gronk Nicandro

To my friends Sue Knussen (In Memoriam) and Anthony Fogg

AINADAMAR
(Fountain of Tears)

David Henry Hwang

Osvaldo Golijov
Edited by Arturo Rodríguez

Preludio de Agua y Caballo
TACET

IMÁGEN I - MARIANA
1. Balada I

* For the Ballads: Open air singing, non vibrato, as if in the streets of Granada. Don't emphasize the dotted rhythms at the expense of the line's thrust. Drive always forward towards the very end of the last note of each phrase. Some heterophony is desired, and freedom in the ornamentation. The grace-notes are gutural.

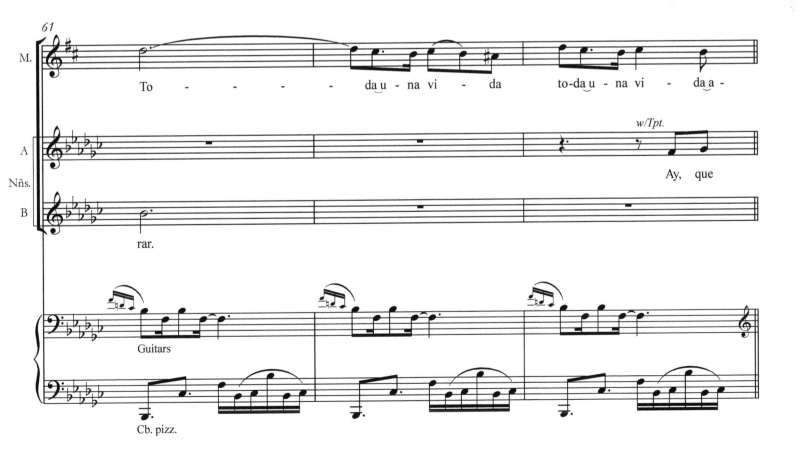

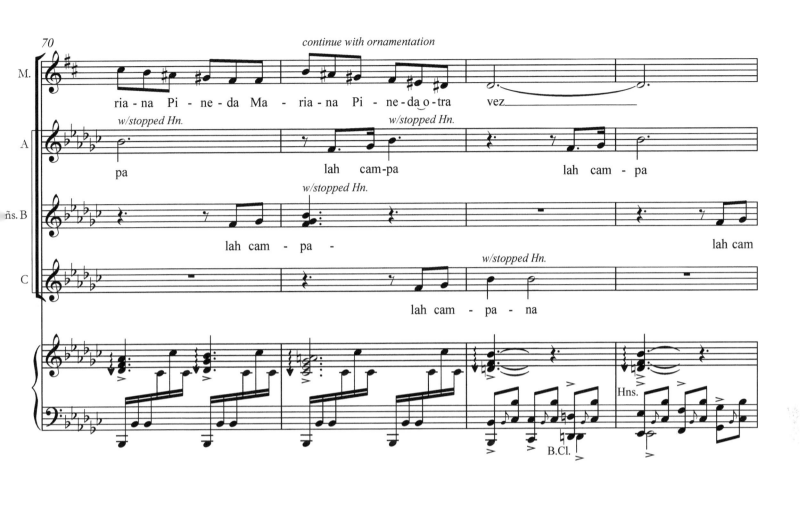

2. Mariana, Tus Ojos

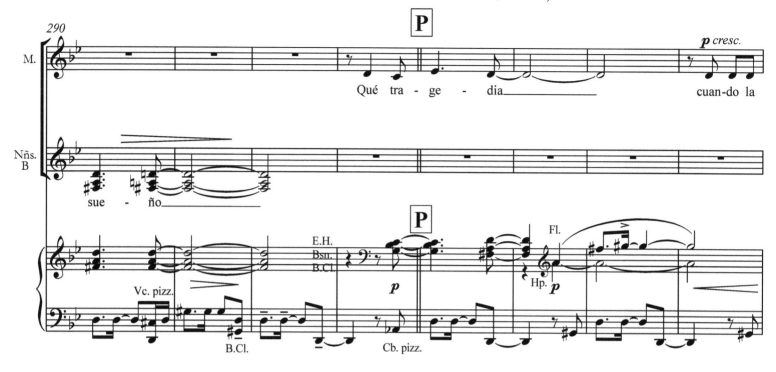

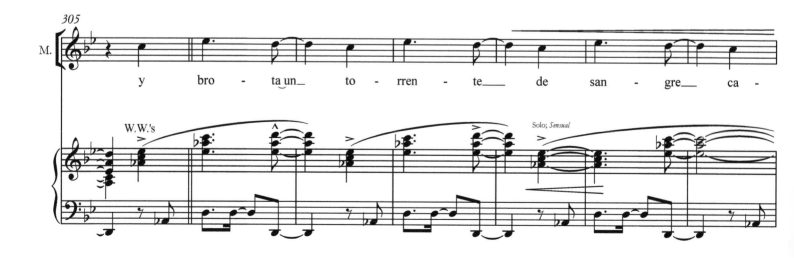

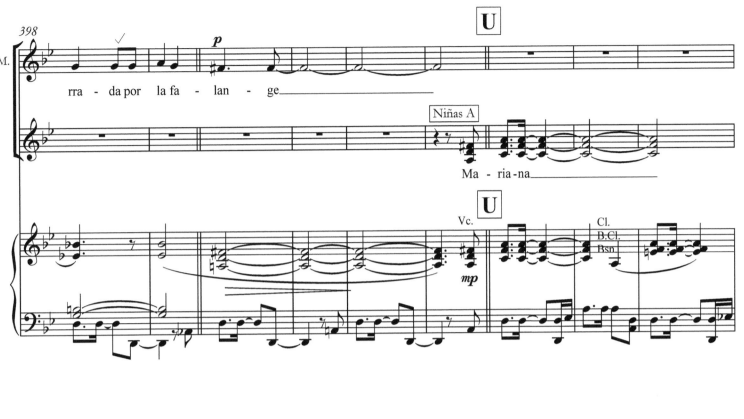

IMÁGEN I - Mariana / 3. Bar "Albor de Madrid"
Chorus TACET

IMÁGEN I - Mariana / 4. Desde mi ventana

IMÁGEN II - FEDERICO

1. Balada II

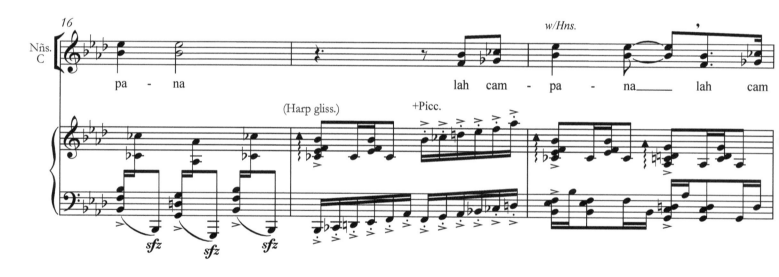

5. Arresto

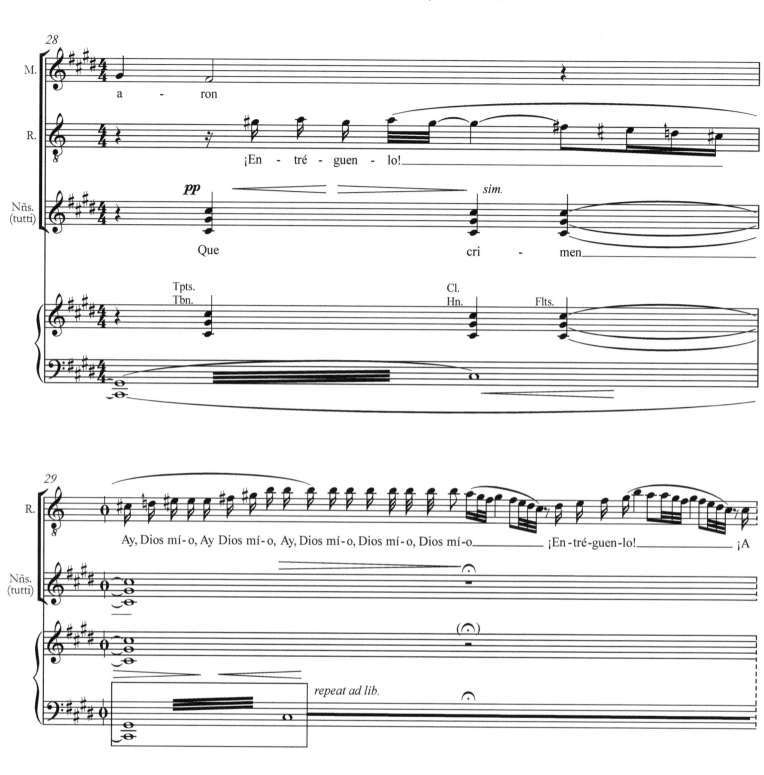

attacca

6. La Fuente de las Lágrimas

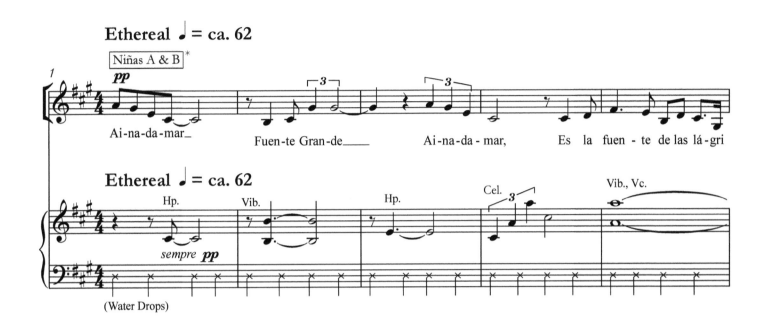

* NOTE TO SOUND PERSON: Add abundant reverb. to "Niñas", so they sound "underwater".

(Water Drops continue sim.)

attacca

7. Confesión

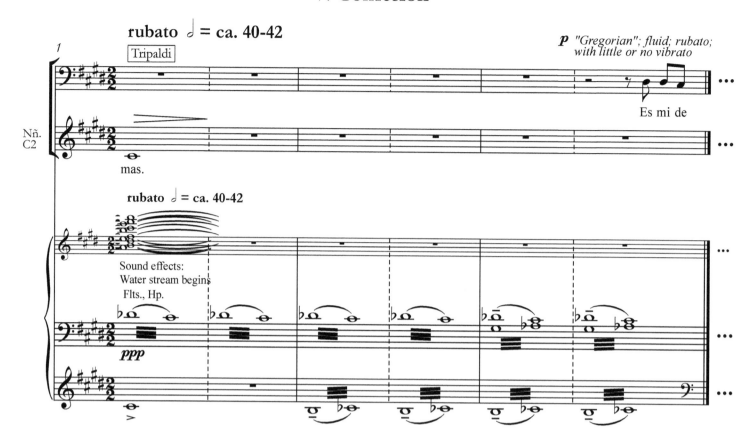

Interludio de Balazos /
Lamento por la Muerte de Federico

TACET

IMÁGEN III - MARGARITA

1. Balada III - Laberinto

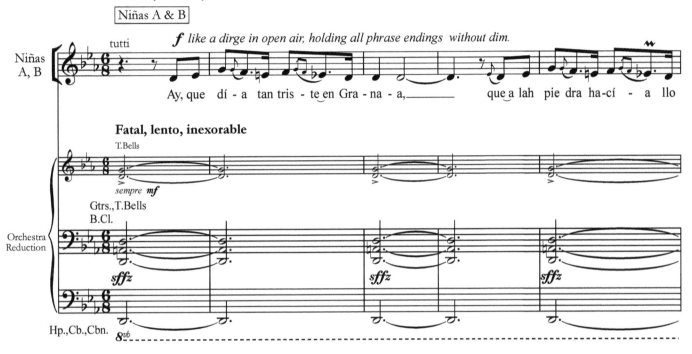

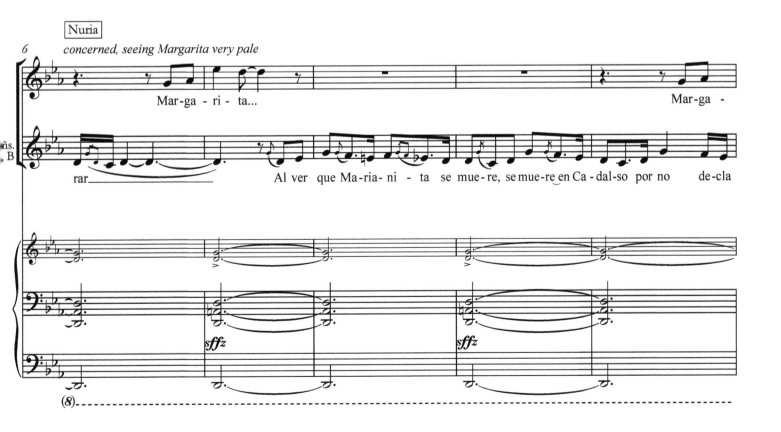

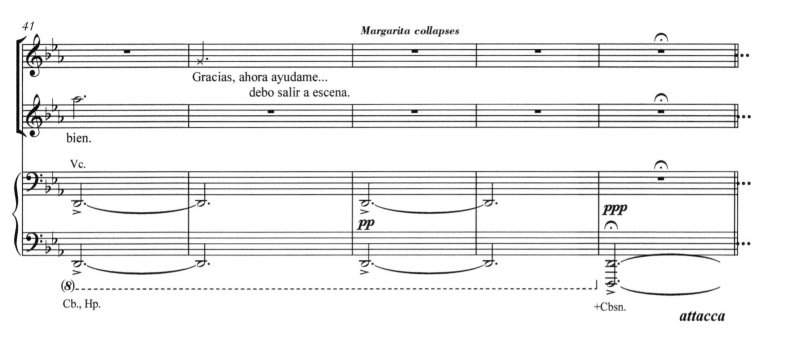

Margarita collapses

Gracias, ahora ayudame...
debo salir a escena.

bien.

Vc.

pp

ppp

(8)

Cb., Hp.

+Cbsn.

attacca

3. Tome su mano

Mismo tempo

Nuria

w/Celesta

Ven - ga, to - me su ma - no   llé - ve - la a su la -

Niñas B

ven - ga___   y

Mismo tempo

Cel.

p

Sound effects: Horse Bridle continues

Cl./Hns.
Hp.   Vib.

dolce

E.H.

p "echo"

Vla.

E.H.

Vc.
Cb. *p*

4. Crepúsculo Delirante

IMÁGEN III - Margarita / 4. Crepúsculo Delirante

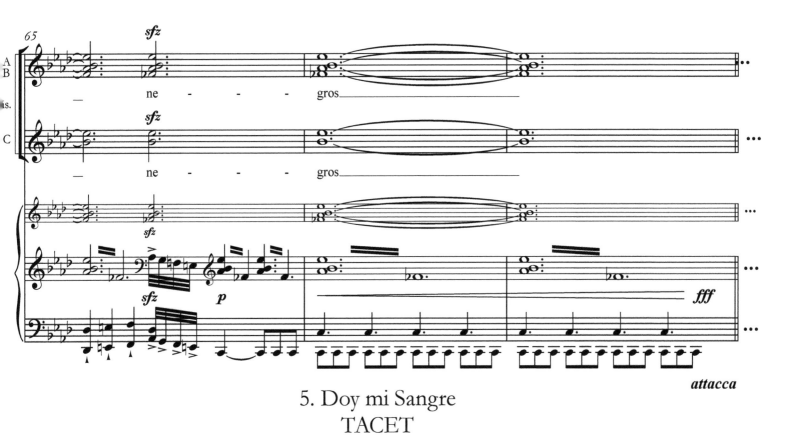

ne - gros

ne - gros

attacca

5. Doy mi Sangre
TACET

6. Yo Soy La Libertad

Yo soy el ma-nan-tial   soy la Li-ber- tad

colla parte

he - ri - da   y   san - gran - do es - pe -

colla parte

IMÁGEN III - Margarita / 6. Yo Soy La Libertad

IMÁGEN III - Margarita / 6. Yo Soy La Libertad

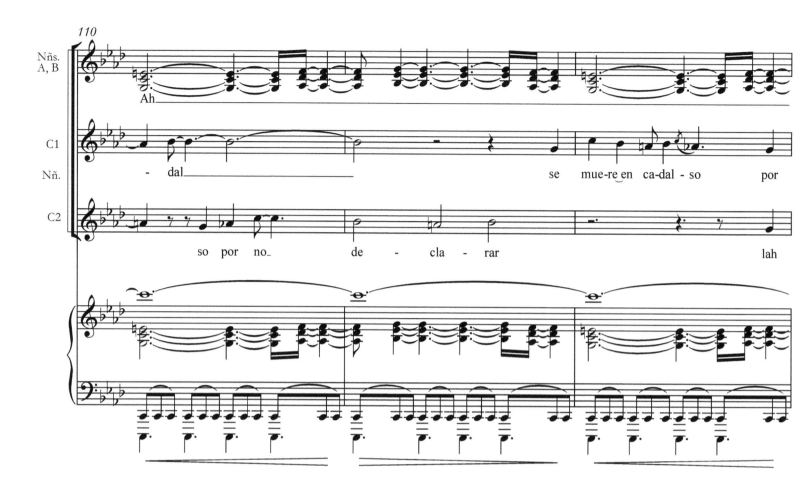

Water Begins

**Hold; Under
Water Postlude***

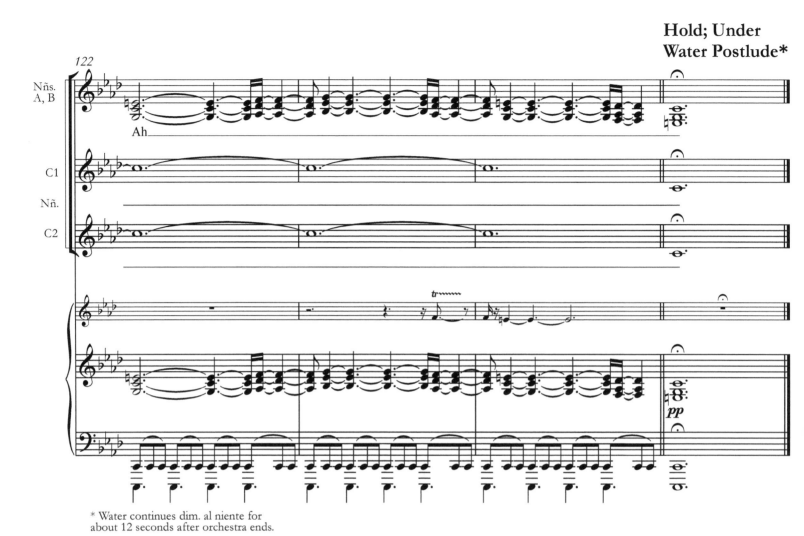

* Water continues dim. al niente for
about 12 seconds after orchestra ends.